Emotions

The Top 100 Best Ways To Gain Emotional Prosperity

By Ace McCloud

Disclaimer

The information provided in this book is designed to provide helpful information on the subjects discussed. This book is not meant to be used, nor should it be used, to diagnose or treat any medical condition. For diagnosis or treatment of any medical problem, consult your own physician. The publisher and author are not responsible for any specific health or allergy needs that may require medical supervision and are not liable for any damages or negative consequences from any treatment, action, application or preparation, to any person reading or following the information in this book. Any references included are provided for informational purposes only. Readers should be aware that any websites or links listed in this book may change.

Table of Contents

DEDICATED TO THOSE WHO ARE PLAYING THE GAME OF LIFE TO

WIN

KEEP ON PUSHING AND NEVER GIVE UP!

Ace McCloud

Be sure to check out my website for all my Books and Audio books.

www.AcesEbooks.com

Introduction

Do you find it hard to focus on what you wish to achieve and bring it to fruition? The chances are that if this is happening to you that you will find that it is your emotions that are getting in the way of your achieving the life and happiness you deserve.

Do you often feel exhausted, overwhelmed, stressed out, or anxious? Do you find yourself struggling to keep up because you feel tired all the time due to a lack of refreshing sleep, because of all the worries that flood into your head as soon as it hits the pillow?

It doesn't have to be that way. I have compiled *The Top 100 Best Ways to Gain Emotional Prosperity* for you, so that you can find the techniques that will work best for you as you gain emotional mastery; and use your emotions to improve your everyday life. This book will show you just how easy it can be to learn the skills required to get your emotions working for you rather than against you, and help you to build a fulfilling and enjoyable lifestyle.

I have written and researched many books on self help and personal growth, and have put into action all the tools and techniques I learn with every book I write. Therefore, as you read this book you can be assured that every tip and technique in this book has been proven to work. I have also worked directly with clients to help them to implement the tools within this book so that they too can improve their lives and improve their emotional prosperity.

Many people from all walks of life - from entrepreneurs wanting to improve their productivity, to students feeling overwhelmed by the pressure of examinations; busy Moms who don't have enough time in the day, to people suffering from depression and anxiety – all can benefit from the knowledge included within this helpful guide. You can read it cover to cover, or simply dip in when you need to. There is bound to be something in here that will help you tackle and get on top of your emotions.

Recently I worked with Becky, a busy woman who felt completely overwhelmed by her work and family commitments. She often found herself getting angry over the tiniest of things and wished to be in better command of her emotions, as she felt it was impacting on her relationships with others. We spent some time implementing some of the tools in this book. She found it really beneficial to understand how to recognize the changes in her body as she became stressed. By simply learning how her body felt, she was able to notice before she snapped at her colleagues and family. This allowed her to take a step back and start to understand what her triggers were. Once she knew what these were, she was able to prepare better for situations when she knew they may arise, or found ways to avoid them where she could. Michael, a teenager in college, was very anxious – especially around girls. He really wanted to be more relaxed and confident amongst his peers. We used some of the exercises in this book to help him to do just that. Within a month he had enjoyed his first date with a young woman and was looking forward to a second one with her last time we were in touch.

I promise you that if you just put one or two of these techniques into practice on a daily basis that you will feel happier and more confident. If you implement five to ten you will improve your life considerably, and if you make twenty or more a regular part of your daily routine your life will change dramatically. Your health and mood will improve, you will have more energy, and you will enjoy more prosperity and success every day.

So, don't hang around here! Now is the time to learn how to master and make use of your anger, to turn around your anxiety and negative thinking and to build the life you deserve. You can enjoy your life just the way it is – there is no need for expensive gadgets; a better job; or even a more perfect relationship. Everything you need to improve your life is in you, and you can get at it by using this book and taking action on what you read.

The tools and techniques that are outlined in this book have been proven to get positive and long lasting results. Just keep reading, take action on each technique, work out which ones have the most impact for you as an individual and then make them a part of a daily routine that will have you enjoying your life more and more every day. Each technique can be used as a standalone – or can be combined with any of the others. Just enjoy reading, enjoy experimenting, and have fun as you realize that your emotions can be used to create an incredible life.

Chapter 1: Why Our Emotions Are So Important

Many of us have actually begun to be a little scared of our emotions. We live in a world that encourages us to never fully show the full spectrum of our emotions. It would seem that it is okay for us to show the positive emotions of happiness, confidence, joy and success; but it is frowned upon that we are sad, or depressed and anxious. So called 'negative' emotions are seen as unhelpful or even dangerous and too many people try to internalize these, rather than expressing them or taking action when they feel them. You may have swallowed down anger, or forced back tears on many an occasion yourself. Science is showing us now just how dangerous this can be; that suppressing any emotion can have a negative effect on our wellbeing.

But we still teach our children not to show anger. We still teach them that big boys and girls don't cry. I have lost count of the amount of people I have worked with over the years who see it as weakness to admit that they need to cry, and will deny that they ever feel angry. This is crazy – we all need to let our emotions run their course. If we give ourselves permission to feel, then they can serve their purpose, we can learn from them and move on. However if we trap them inside they will continue to repeat on us, until we finally have to notice them. This can mean that a moment of frustration can turn into a lifetime of bitter, repressed, passive-aggressive behaviors – driving people from us and leaving us extremely lonely and unhappy. Yet had we just expressed our frustration at the time we felt it, and taken a moment to analyze that emotion, we could have found out which of our rules had been broken - by us or by somebody else - and then established if it was a rule or value that we need to keep or dismiss, especially if it may continue to throw up the same problem again and again.

We live in a world where emotional health and wellbeing are often ignored and dismissed. Many people suffering from treatable conditions like depression will not go to their doctors because they do not wish to suffer the stigma of having a mental health condition. Yet, that same person would more than happily go if they had digestive problems or headaches to get medication and treatment. The sad fact is that many of the physical health problems that we all suffer these days – from a simple cold, through to cancer and other life threatening conditions - are all affected by our emotional health. Recently I read that physicians believe that around 80-95% of all medical problems that they treat regularly are caused by stress. This is why it is so vital to make sure that you take care not just of your physical health, but your mental health too.

Whether you suffer from a mental health condition or are blissfully free of one right now, you still have a mental health state; in the same way that whether you have the presence of a physical illness or not, that you have a physical health state. That state may currently be good, mediocre, or terrible – but it is there nonetheless! Like so many things in life, your emotional prosperity will depend on you accepting that you have emotions. Some emotions feel good, some not so good, and others feel downright unpleasant. This does not make any of them good emotions, or bad emotions. They are all just emotions.

I will try not to use the terms 'positive' or 'negative', 'good' or bad' in regards to emotions in this book, because the only things that differentiate between emotions are how they make us feel; and how we choose to act upon them. Put simply, our 'use' of an emotion, the way we think about it, and let it manifest in our life, is what will give it a positive or negative impact in our life – the individual emotion itself cannot do this alone. Emotions do not have any morality – they just are, so the idea that a certain emotion makes us a better person, or that another makes us a terrible one is also a concept that we need to try to move away from. Sadness is an essential pre-requisite so that we understand when we are happy; anger can prompt us into taking incredible action to right injustice; anxiety can give us the heads up that we have deep commitment to something or someone; frustration can help us to change our beliefs and values so that they support us better.

It is impossible to be happy and content all of the time. If you were, you would never know that there was any other way to feel if this was the case. In the same way that our body will give us pain to let us know when there is something we need to change; our mind will send us an emotion. We need to learn to use these warning signals better – not try to eradicate them from our lives. Many of my clients over the years have come with just one goal – to be happy. I have to very patiently explain to them that they may well get over their anxiety and depression, but this does not mean that they will be permanently happy, and never experience an unpleasant emotion ever again. Good and bad things will happen to you every day of your life – how you feel about your life overall will depend on how you focus and use these events. As Shakespeare has Hamlet say in the play of the same name "There is nothing good or bad but thinking makes it so."

Hopefully the techniques you will learn in the next few chapters will help you to get the most from every emotion you ever feel, so that you can learn to take control of your emotions and put them to the best use. It is important to realize that it is your emotions and your thoughts which are currently creating your life; they are directly responsible for whether you find the success you want, or are achieving a life of ill health and 'failure' at every turn. If you would like a little bit more information about how our emotions change our lives, check out this great YouTube video called "How to Master and Control Your Emotions" by Actualized.org, because we are going to move swiftly on to some incredible techniques that will help you to change your focus and change your life.

Chapter 2: Get Aware And You Can Change Your Life

The first section of Techniques and tools are all about gaining awareness of our emotions. Without awareness you cannot change anything, so it is the obvious starting point.

#1 You will get whatever you focus on!

It is really important to be aware that our thoughts direct the results that we will achieve. If your focus is on the wrong thing, then you won't get the results that you desire. This is a simple exercise that will help you to see exactly how you focus on different aspects of your life.

1. Firstly I want you to think about an aspect of your life that makes you happy or makes you smile. Just write a paragraph about it, don't check what you write, just write for a few minutes. This could be about your relationship, or your job, maybe your home – anything as long as it makes you happy and gives you pleasure.

2. Now, think of an area of your life that isn't going so well and write a paragraph about that. This could be an aspect of your job, maybe things aren't going too well in your family for some reason.

3. Now I want you to break each paragraph down into definite statements. For example "I love my husband" or "my children are beautiful." Some of your sentences may contain more than one statement, so they may end up as a number of now shorter options. I do this with neon highlighters. I want you to highlight any statements that are saying pleasant things about the subject, or are about the emotions you enjoy feeling in one color and any less than kind or unpleasant feeling emotions in a contrasting one.

4. You should notice that each statement will probably have a similar ratio of color spread throughout it – though in the first paragraph the higher number should be the statements that make you feel all warm and fuzzy, and in the second paragraph the number of not so nice statements will be the higher of the two – though both will probably have at least one of the opposing type.

Hopefully this exercise will have shown you that there is a definite ratio of pleasurable and not so nice when you think about something you love, and something you dislike. This is a ratio that you will find very useful when you are trying to change your emotions – as it points out that you can still have a few unpleasant thoughts even about the things you love the most!

#2 Define your emotions very carefully!

This is a step that so many of us forget to do accurately. There is a massive difference between feeling a bit peeved about something; and being furious about it. Sadly, this can mean that we don't often use the correct word to describe our emotion. This often means that it will make us feel worse than we might expect, or will negate just how unhappy we may feel, as we also have a tendency to underplay other emotions - saying we are just frustrated when we are truly fuming; or are a bit sad when we feel heartbroken – or the worst of all, that we are fine, when in reality we feel utterly terrible.

So, make a really long list of emotional words using a thesaurus and check their meanings in the dictionary. The longer your list the better, then when you give your emotion a name in future you can be careful to use the correct label! You can try and tick off at least 15 different emotions each day if you want. Most of us tend to only use a very small vocabulary to describe how we feel – make your life more accurate and more vivid with the correct words to describe how you truly feel.

You can maybe even make a small, credit card sized card with a broad selection of emotions (use both sides!) so that, if you are out and about and not near a dictionary, you can scan your list of words for the one that fits the situation best. If you are a bit low, great – don't call yourself depressed. If you are angry great – don't call yourself annoyed. Be honest with yourself about how you actually feel.

#3 How Do You Actually Feel Right Now?

We can often be a little unaware of our emotional environment. Try to get into the habit of checking in. Pay attention to how you feel – physically and emotionally. Are you feeling tense or relaxed? Do you have any fear or distress? Are you feeling confident and strong? This is so simple, but can be such a useful tool, and it will help you to build up awareness. Without awareness you may never realize what it is you need to tweak – which beliefs or values you hold might be holding you back. Create some quick feedback loops!

If you are finding lots of the same, flat emotions such as boredom; feeling 'fine'; or 'I'm okay' then use exercise 2 above to make sure you can learn to pinpoint your emotions more accurately. Take time today to check in every ten to fifteen minutes and just ask non-judgmentally how you are feeling in that moment.

#4 Mindfulness Meditation

This is a very specific form of meditation that is all about taking notice of how you feel in the moment. Mindfulness meditations don't need to take long – about 5 minutes or so to get started is all it will take. Check in two or three times a day. You may find that this is all you ever need, but research has shown that the greatest benefits from this technique can be felt if you can build it up to 20 to 30 minutes each time.

I know some people who like to do this when they go out for a walk, but I think to get started it is easier to sit somewhere peaceful and start by noticing your breath as it enters and leaves your body. Then turn your attention to how your physical body feels. Finally focus on your emotional feelings in that moment. Don't make any judgments, just let the thoughts come and go, and do not try to fix anything!

If you want a hand to help you to get started you might wish to try this YouTube video "Mindfulness Meditation in Twenty Minutes" by Michael Sealey.

#5 What Have You Done Today?

Many of us have a horrible tendency to bully ourselves: we tell ourselves that we are useless and don't achieve enough; or we may say horrible things about the way that we look or feel – often the things we tell ourselves are completely untrue.

This little exercise will help you to realize just how much you actually do in a single 24 hour period. Simply write down everything in a journal. From the moment you open your eyes, tune in every ten to fifteen minutes and record what you have done in that time, and how you feel about it. This will not only help you to realize that you are far more productive than you give yourself credit for; but will help you to realize that there are many moments of achievement, happiness, joy etc. as well as boredom, or frustration. We can all too easily have one bad thing happen, and base our emotions about our day around that one single thing – when the rest of the day has actually been pretty splendid!

#6 Get Connected to your body!

When we get stressed or anxious, feel frustrated, happy or joyful, we will feel certain physical sensations throughout our body. From clenched and tight muscles, to rapid breathing, bloating and many other symptoms, our body will react to our emotional state and provide the physical state that it believes corresponds with it. This can be a really useful tool for us to use, as it means that we can change our emotions quite literally in a moment.

I want you to imagine that you are feeling depressed. I want you to let your body do what you think a depressed body would display to the world. Assume the posture, sit how a depressed person would sit, walk how you think they might walk, talk in the way you think that they may talk. Now, I want you to try and smile and be cheerful in that position. It is quite difficult to do isn't it?

Now, I want you to assume your most confident and happy posture. Arrange your limbs and torso in the way that represents confidence to you. Sit confidently, walk confidently, talk confidently. Now try and be sad and miserable whilst maintaining that posture!

This exercise shows us just how linked our emotions are to our physical state, so spend some time working out what the physical states are that match the emotions you wish to feel more of – and just put your body into those positions as often as you can.

#7 Bodily Sensations Make Great Warning Systems!

Following on from the previous tip, we can use our physical symptoms to help us to know when a bad mood or stressful occurrence may affect our behaviour. By understanding and spotting the early warning signals that occur in our bodies we can take control of the situation more quickly.

Do you feel your muscles tightening up; do you start to get stomach cramps; lose your appetite; or notice your breathing getting shallower and more rapid? Maybe you get headaches; or lower back pain. You may notice yourself becoming louder and more agitated; or quieter and more withdrawn. You may even freeze and find it difficult to feel or do anything.

Once you can spot your stress response, you can look for the early warning signs. The earlier you spot that you are having a negative reaction to something or someone, the more likely you will be to be able to back track and find out what triggered the response. It will also mean that you can change the way you feel more quickly than if you let the emotion or situation get out of hand.

#8 Choose The Techniques That Will Suit Your Reaction Best!

Being the individuals that we are - with different pressures and strains, and different ways of doing things - it is key to choose techniques that suit you and your predominant learning styles, and sensory dominance.

Most of the best ways to help combat stress and the more unpleasant emotions will involve one or more of our senses – so by understanding your most dominant senses you will be able to choose suitable techniques to help you to relax and restore balance. Visual types will maybe enjoy surrounding themselves with beauty: art galleries; stunning images; magnificent landscapes etc. Those who respond well to smell may wish to bake or have an aromatherapy massage. A kinaesthetic person may enjoy a massage, getting out into their garden, or making things with their hands. An auditory person may enjoy attending a concert or listening to a favourite piece of music, even to birdsong or speaking to a favourite friend.

If you are someone who reacts with aggressive, loud behaviours you need to find techniques that will assist you in relaxing and calming down. However if you tend to go quiet and introverted when faced with emotional distress you may need to find techniques that are more stimulating and will bring you out of your shell. If you tend to freeze, you may need comfort and stimulation to assist you to feel better and more in control of the situation.

#9 Be Aware of Your Inner Dialogue

As we have already mentioned, we are what we think, so it is very important to ensure that the thoughts we think are supportive to our health and wellbeing.

I want you to take one day, and just notice how often you repeat a single unsupportive statement – for example "I am tired" or "I am so bored". Choose something that is the most relevant to you – the thing you most wish to not be a part of your life going forward.

The number that you have accumulated through the day will give you a rough idea of how many times you keep this single, unhelpful, phrase running around your head. For many of my clients this number has been in the hundreds! This gives you an idea of the scope of the problem – if you are repeating this one statement that many times, what about all the others? Also, what about all the times you may have repeated this without actually spotting that you had done so?

This anomaly in what we can consciously detect, and how many times we actually make statements that support results we don't really want is what often makes using affirmations so difficult. The amount of times that would be required to consciously repeat the affirmation to over-ride the repetition we have been making over many years – plus trying to make sure we no longer say the old statement - is an incredibly time consuming and difficult thing to do –that doesn't mean that affirmations aren't useful, they are, but like so many of the techniques in this book they are best used in combination with other options.

#10 Secret Saboteurs

There are a small group of words that can cause all kinds of problems for us when we are trying to build a healthy and prosperous emotional life. These include *but; can't; won't; must; don't; and; should; would;* and finally *if.*

These words can be very dangerous as they can imply certain premise' to our brains. Like our choice of vocabulary to describe our emotions, the way we use these words to link concepts can be very damaging to our emotional prosperity.

> *But* is a little word, and it would appear to have little real meaning. However, if somebody says "I like you, but I think you should tone down your attitude a bit" they have in essence said that they don't like our attitude. Therefore the first part of the sentence has been obliterated by

the second clause. How many people do you genuinely like who you think have a bad attitude? *But* says that whatever came first in the statement isn't true, so be very careful how you use it.

And is a linking word that we all use a lot. Many of us will write out lists of what we want – be it a shopping list or a goal list – and in our mind we will link the words upon it with *and*. Now, if your goal is to feel happy and prosperous and your list of 40 things that might make you feel that way is linked with *and* you are going to be waiting a very long time before you can manifest everything on that list. That means you will be waiting a really long time before you feel happy and prosperous right? So, when you use lists, try using *or* instead to link your requirements – that way you can feel happy and prosperous if you achieve even a single thing that is on that list!

Can't is all about shutting off possibility, as are *won't* and *don't*. *Can't* is so final that it completely blocks your brain from coming up with an alternative route – even if you really want to find one - but all of them will restrict and reduce your ability to get the result you claim to desire.

Simply put, maybe you feel that a task is really tricky, and will take a lifetime to master – but that doesn't actually make it impossible – therefore you *can* do it! Maybe you *won't* do something, but this doesn't mean that you aren't capable of doing it if you chose to!

Be honest with yourself about this – we can all do anything that any other human on this planet can; what makes us different is our desire to do so, and how much effort we are prepared to put in to learning a particular skill or ability.

Must, would and *should* are also tricky for us. There are truly very few things that we actually *must* do in order to survive – breathe; drink; sleep; and eat, that is it! Everything we do outside of these four is a choice. If you find your day is populated by things you feel have as much importance to keep you alive as these four ('I must go to work; I must get to the shops; I must get the ironing complete' etc) then you are not surprisingly likely to be prone to stress and overwhelm.

Ironically most of us pay more attention to the things that are choices, than the things that are really genuine *musts* in life. If we put as much effort into ensuring we get those four right as we do the things that we claim are, then we would be healthier, happier and lead more balanced lives!

Would and *should* imply that we will feel guilty if we do not do the things that follow them and so they not only make us stressed trying to complete them, but we tell ourselves that we are terrible people if we don't do them.

They are lesser cousins of *must* but they really can make us feel pretty unhappy and inadequate.

Finally in this section comes *if*. *If* is a very unfortunate little word; *if* implies that we are too lazy to do whatever it is that we think we should be doing, achieving or being. It is also the word that implies regret. 'If only I had done that' is such a common refrain; 'if I had the time I would...' These statements aren't just unhelpful, they are pointless. You either did, or you didn't; you either will or you won't. Don't make excuses, don't have regrets!

By being careful around your use of these words, making sure you use them as infrequently as you can you will find your emotional prosperity and your physical wellbeing will start to improve. If you choose not to do something that is fine, but please be kind to yourself about that choice – no more bullying, no more excuses, they simply aren't needed. If you want to do something else, just do it!

#11 What Are You Focused On?

When we begin to work on making changes in our lives we often tend to set our goals around the things we don't wish to have or be any more. "I don't want to be stuck in this dead end job" or maybe "I wish I didn't have to do so much housework anymore."

We need to remember that our brains can be very clever and a little daft at times too. Our brains focus on the objects of statements, and if we are focusing on our ill health, or our rubbish job – rather than the health and vitality we desire or the great new job we would love – then we will just get more of what we focus upon. Check that you are focusing on what you actually want – not what you don't!

#12 Do You Run from Pain, Or Towards Pleasure?

This may seem an odd question, but it is really important to understand which of these two motivators is most prominent within your personality. Many people will automatically say that they wish to move towards pleasure, but in reality we are far more programmed to move away from pain. This is why many of us find it difficult to make healthful changes until a doctor tells us our lives are at massive risk.

Knowing this will help you to select the right techniques for you. Visualization, for example, will work for those who love to move towards pleasure; whereas NLP techniques such as 'The Cinema' may work better for those who run from pain as it ramps up the pain to get you to take action.

#13 Whose Standards Are You Holding Yourself To?

This may be an odd question, and you are possibly yelling "Mine, obviously!" But are you really? So many of the rules we set for ourselves have been inherited without our realizing it.

Do you feel your house must be spotless? Why? I'll be prepared to guess that Mom, or maybe your Grandma had a home that was immaculate. Does it truly matter to you whether your house is as clean as their home was? Remember that they probably didn't have to hold down a job and take care of their home and children – they were her only job. In our crazy world where most homes need both partners to be earning it is difficult to maintain that level of care – but does it really matter to you?

I don't know anybody who comes to see me for my immaculate house – they would be too disappointed. My friends and family come to see me. Frankly, there are more important things I could be doing!

When you feel you have not lived up to some impossible standard, ask where it comes from. Whose voice do you hear telling you it isn't enough? Is it true? Does it even matter to you at all?

#14 What Are Your Priorities?

This tip goes hand in hand with the one above. If you know what your priorities are, then you can ensure that you are putting your efforts into what matters most to you.

My priorities are these: my health; my happiness; my family's health and happiness; my friends; my work; my house and possessions. This means that if I run out of time to get the housework done, or the decorating, then that it fine – as long as I was doing the things that come ahead of it on my list.

Work out your priorities. You may find that currently you are putting too much effort into things that really don't have that much importance to you and your wellbeing. Just have a little play with this, move things around so you choose things that get you hyped up and raring to go!

#15 What Do You Actually Enjoy Doing?

Do you know anymore? Have you managed to put everything you love on hold in order to bring up your children, forge a successful career and always be there for everybody else? So many of my clients come to me with lists of things they feel they 'should' be doing, or 'must' be doing, but forget all about the things that actually make them feel great, be it physically, emotionally or spiritually.

Start making a list and get everything that you can possibly think of that you love doing on there. From the super simple – looking at pictures of people you love or giggling at a daft cat on YouTube – to the majestic. Whatever you enjoy, have ever enjoyed, or may ever enjoy can go on this list.

Now do at least two things that are on this list every single day!

Chapter 3: How You Can Take Control of Your Emotions

Now you are aware of how much your inner - and outer dialogue - may be messing with your emotional and physical equilibrium, it is time to start finding ways to take control of your emotions. There are a lot of tools and techniques to do this, I have picked the very best ones for you to include here.

#16 Pick Your Battles Wisely

We all find ourselves in arguments or disagreements from time to time. One of the best ways I have found to lessen my emotional burden is to pick and choose the fights that are worth having.

Most of the time my need to be right, is much less than my need to maintain a relationship with someone I care about, and so I have learnt to let things slide at times even when I know I am right! Just because somebody disagrees with me doesn't make my being right any less true.

It is not my role here on earth to ensure that everybody agrees with me, in fact it would be a pretty dull place to live in if it was – but I am here to make my own experience better. If that means letting my Mom win so I maintain the peace; or allowing a so-called expert tell me something and then go and do it my way then that is fine.

I do not have to win every battle I face, I don't even have to fight every battle that is put before me - in fact I don't have to look at my life as a series of battles at all. A wise person once told me this fantastic affirmation: "My way is not THE way; it is just MY way." Remembering this, and how much I care about the person who may not agree with me, helps me to keep my cool and just agree to disagree with them.

#17 Talk To Someone You Trust

Many of us are busy looking after everyone else, are always there when friends or family need us – and yet consider it weakness to ask for help ourselves. I want you to take a moment now and think about how you feel when you help others.

I will make a little prediction here – helping others makes you feel great! Makes you feel all warm and fuzzy, proud and connected to help someone you love right?

This feeling is a gift that we are given by the generosity of our friends or family as they open up and allow us into their lives to help them out. It makes us feel powerful, benevolent, content and downright useful. So quit hoarding the good stuff and let someone you love feel that fantastic for helping you out too!

#18 Try And See The Funny Side!

Laughter truly is great medicine. This YouTube video "Norman Cousins, An Anatomy of An Illness" by C. J. Mason is a small excerpt of a longer interview with Norman Cousins, about his findings regarding laughter and its ability to heal, also detailed in his book.

Have you ever noticed how much children smile and laugh? They deal with emotions so much better than we do – partly because we permit them to do so, but also because they know that those emotions are fleeting. They will cry their hearts out when they fall and scrape a knee to release the pain, then twenty minutes later will be laughing their head off at a cartoon.

We've all heard the phrase "You'll look back and laugh at this one day", so why not laugh about it now! For information on this topic, be sure to check out my book on Laughter Therapy.

#19 Confidence Building

Confidence is a key aspect of emotional prosperity. It isn't easy to maintain when we bully ourselves daily; so in order to help us to do this, spend some time every day if you can - but at a minimum once a week - listing your strengths; the things you have done well; skills you have learnt; skills you have improved upon; and the positive things that have been said to you by others.

#20 Accept Compliments Gracefully

This sounds like a minor thing, but there is a key difference between the way a person who has mastered their emotions deals with a compliment, and the way someone who hasn't does.

The person with emotional mastery will accept the compliment with a grateful heart. They do not feel the need to deflect it with a return compliment; they do not feel the need to be bashful or uncomfortable and try to ignore it. They say thank you for the gift that they have been given.

Next time someone offers you a kind word, don't auto pilot into saying how much you love their shoes, or try and hide. Say a simple, heartfelt thank you.

#21 Journaling

Journaling is a technique that has so much power when we wish to improve our experiences in life. For some reason getting our thoughts out onto paper and in black and white can make it so much easier to process and analyse them more rationally. Just a few minutes a day can help you to spot patterns before they become problematic, and therefore because you spot things early this means that you can take the actions you need to, to ensure you remain balanced and well.

#22 Reframe Your Experiences

This is a technique used within Neuro Linguistic Programming (NLP) to help us to take the sting out of things. Essentially you take a situation that is causing you concern and you try and make it easier to cope with.

For example a busy Mom, who has had a horrible day at work, may feel overwhelmed by everything she has to do when she gets home. Her thoughts are:

"I am so tired, and I have to get the house clean and tidy before my husband gets home, I need to get the kids bathed, get their tea and get them fed and off to bed, make sure there is a decent dinner for Paul, and then I have to clean the kitchen. Oh and I must get all the ironing finished as I need that blouse for my interview tomorrow."

Now, though it may feel imperative that she personally undertake all of these tasks before she gets to bed that night, I hope you can see that there are some that aren't entirely essential – on a night when she is tired, before an interview that she wants to go well in particular. Her husband could maybe help her to clean and tidy the house once he gets in while she feeds and bathes the children before bed. She only really needs one blouse ironed, so the entire pile could wait until another time when she has more energy or time. So a reframe of this situation could be:

"I will call Paul and ask him to come in early tonight if he can as I need a hand with a few chores. If he can sort out the house while I get the kids fed and off to bed, and maybe he could just iron that one blouse for me while I fix our dinner and clean the kitchen afterwards."

Everything, which needs to, still gets done but it is a much less frantic task for our busy Mom. However, it could be reframed even further to take even more pressure off:

"I'll call Paul and ask him to pick up some food to go from that great new healthy restaurant tonight for dinner so nobody has to cook. He can feed the kids while I iron my blouse, then we can bathe them and put them to bed and relax. I'll do the rest of the housework tomorrow after my interview."

#23 Get Grateful

In order to be happier and healthier, all the current research seems to show that our most powerful tool is getting grateful. We already have so many wonderful things in our lives, things that we dismiss within a few hours of gaining them. Spend some time every day thinking about all the wonderful things you already have, and you will see your life improve – and I can guarantee that because what you focus on is what you get in life, that when you focus on the good stuff in your life, you will get more good stuff to be grateful for! You can check out my book on gratitude to really get in depth knowledge and skills for doing this.

#24 Learn To Like Yourself As You Are

This is quite a tough ask, particularly when we feel a little low. The simple truth is that we care and nurture people we love, or at least like! So if you currently don't like yourself very much you probably aren't bothering to take the steps you would to care for somebody you do love.

Take a few seconds to contemplate the levels of understanding, care and affection you lavish on the people in your life that you truly love. If you are having troubles emotionally, I would be willing to bet that you don't even class yourself as deserving of the level of care and attention that you would give a stranger, let alone someone you love.

If you would make the effort to cook a wholesome meal for anyone else in your life, you need to do it for yourself. If you would forgive a friend for something they have said or done, you need to give yourself the same compassion.

None of us is perfect – so make sure you hold yourself accountable in the same way you would somebody you love. Treat yourself with respect and love and you may find that your health improves; your mood improves; your sleep will improve; and your relationships will skyrocket in terms of levels of commitment and connection.

#25 Don't Be A Doormat!

This seemed a natural follow on from the tip above. We all know someone we think of as a bit of a martyr to their job, or their family, or a cause they hold dear. This is fine as long as they balance this with their own needs; and those of others in their life – it is when these martyr like tendencies take over that you need to worry. If you are aware that you are always the first person people turn to when they have a problem, yet never burden others with your issues chances are you are showing a little of this doormat tendency. It is okay to say 'no' occasionally to helping others, especially when doing so puts our own wellbeing at risk.

Remember, if you are a puddle of emotional mush, or have had so long pushing yourself too hard that your body breaks down and gives you a debilitating illness, you will be no use to anyone – try and maintain a balance between your own needs and those of others, that way you can continue to help lots of people over many long happy, and healthy years.

#26 Distance Yourself From Hurtful Situations

Are you in a job you love, or one you hate? Does your home not suit your needs? Do you find yourself spending all your time doing things you don't enjoy, rather than those you love? If so then you may need to have a bit of an environmental overhaul. If we wish to maintain our emotional equilibrium it can be really important to try and make sure there are at least pockets in our lives where we are in places we wish to be.

This could be as simple as stopping procrastinating and actually decorating our homes; maybe looking for a new role in a company where we will be appreciated; or not committing quite so often to spending time doing things we dislike, so we can prioritise those that we do more. It is your life, and it is up to you how you live it.

#27 Distance Yourself From Hurtful People

Some of the people in our lives are easy to commit to the fringes, but some we convince ourselves are not. If your Pop is mean to you, or your Mom constantly puts your efforts down then you are just as justified in relegating them to the edges of your day to day living as you would be a hurtful person you barely know on social media.

Your emotional equilibrium is your responsibility. If you continue to put yourself into a position where others can hurt you, you will find it very difficult to ever pull yourself up out of any funk, you will feel stressed and harassed into eternity.

If you wish to feel good, you need to spend time around people who make you feel good. If you cannot completely remove those who drain your energies from your life, you can at the very least restrict the time you do spend with them, or are in contact with them. If you don't pick up the telephone, or ignore texts from them until you feel that you are in a place to deal with them, they cannot get at you! Then when you choose to call and are feeling positive and in control, you can swiftly move them on from their discontent and onto more positive subjects!

#28 Make Friends With Your Emotions

There is nothing wrong with feeling sad. It doesn't make you a bad person. There is nothing wrong with feeling angry as long as you use your anger and don't let it spill out and hurt others. Bob Geldof went to Africa in the 1980's. What he saw there made him sad and angry. That anger spurred him into organising friends within the music industry to put on a concert and record a song. This was Live Aid, and it became a worldwide phenomenon. Thousands of lives were saved, and continue to be so because of his sadness and anger.

When we make friends with our emotions, and value the more unpleasant ones as much as we do the wonderful ones then we can learn a lot about ourselves and the world we live in. Don't let the emotion take over and paralyse you - use your emotions to help you to improve this crazy world!

#29 Stop, Reflect And Identify!

In order to master your emotions, and have them work for you to create prosperity, you need to be able to Stop; Reflect and Identify. Once you can do this, you are one step closer to establishing what your emotion is telling you; whether you are working in a way that is in tune with your values and beliefs, or in a way that is taking you further away from them. It also makes it easier to spot those values and beliefs that might not be working for you any more – then you can change them or eradicate them to continue on your path more freely.

#30 Your Emotions Are Just Like Aches And Pains

When you are about to get a cold, you probably start to notice a few early warning symptoms. Maybe your joints get a little bit more achy than usual; you may have a sinus headache; or maybe you get a scratchy throat or sneeze more often. These early warning signals mean you can either take evasive action, or get prepared for the cold that is on its way.

Your emotional health has the same early warning signals – you just have to learn what yours are. Before you blow up in anger, or descend into depression you may notice that your body feels more tense; that your breathing gets shallower and more rapid. You may notice that you are a little more snappy about little things, or that you wish to closet yourself away from other people.

The great thing about knowing the early warning signals mean that you can take action and do something about the emotions before they take over!

#31 What Are You Really Anxious About?

When you get to grips with what is really causing you to feel unhappy or anxious, then you can put the situation into perspective. If you are scared about losing a job you love, but are confusing your anxiety with petty details about office politics and how unpleasant the work environment is now, you might find yourself becoming antagonistic to colleagues and being snippy when at work. This can make management think you don't want to be there, so if a reshuffle happens you could well find yourself getting exactly the thing you didn't want.

When you establish the exact cause of your feelings you can take control of the situation. If you genuinely love your job you should be showing management how much you enjoy being a part of the company; how good you are at what you do; and the value you can offer them. You may still lose your job in a reshuffle – but you will get a far better reference to take with you to a new job! A positive outlook will make you more employable where you are, or if you find yourself having to look for a new role. Fear and worry will make you less than you are capable of being, and that will not make you attractive as a prospect to others.

#32 Have You Got Too Much On Your Plate?

When you have too much on your plate, or a task seems overwhelming we can use a technique borrowed from Cognitive Behavioural Therapy, called Chunking.

When you think about going on holiday how do you 'chunk it'? Do you just think, "We're going on holiday"; or do you go through the long list of needs to make it happen? For example "need to go and get some brochures; decide on a destination; pick a hotel; book it; book flights or ferry; ensure the passport are in date and will be with us on time; ensure we have visas; get the jabs we need; check the weather at the time we are going; check we have enough clothes for the type of weather that will be there; ensure we have some just in case in turns; make sure it is all washed and ironed; pack; double check we have everything; eat a proper breakfast before we go; get to the airport on time; make sure the car is parked securely; get checked in at the airport; go through security; wait for the flight; make sure we are at the right gate; find our seats on the plane;......... etc. ad infinitum!

If you look at things as just a big task, and worry that you don't know where to start or how you will remember to do everything, you can chunk it down into more manageable steps – like those in the latter example.

If you tend to look at things in the latter way, chunking can help you to put some of these smaller items into bigger chunks that will make the entire project seem less overwhelming. For example – book the holiday; make sure we have the required paperwork and inoculations for our destination; get packed and to the airport; enjoy!

It is interesting that people tend to have certain tasks in their lives where they need to make things more compact, and others where they need to expand and make it more achievable step by step. Look at how you are currently chunking things in your life – if they seem to cause you emotional discomfort, try chunking them the opposite way!

#33 What Is The Worst That Could Happen?

Sometimes simply looking at the absolute worst case scenario should something go wrong, we can put our feelings about it into better perspective. It is very rare that the extremes of cause and effect occur – usually we are somewhere along a spectrum. By looking at the worst possible option, we can try and imagine how we would cope with that. If we have a plan already in place we can feel confident that we will be able to tackle it should it occur. This will take away most of the anxiety.

#34 Be Grateful That Where You Find Yourself Isn't The Worst Case Scenario

You are still alive, and you are functioning, so the absolute worst has not happened. Get grateful that you are alive, and still able to tackle any problem that comes your way!

#35 Emotional Freedom Techniques

Want to master an emotion or a symptom in just a few moments? EFT is a fantastic technique that can really help you to regain your balance and get you feeling great in just a few minutes. You can get a free manual on how to use this fantastic tapping technique at www.emofree.com Its founder, Gary Craig, takes you through step by step how to use the technique to relieve everything from unpleasant emotions, to physical symptoms, fears and phobias and even very long seated issues in just moments. Or, you can simply go to YouTube and type in the word "Tapping" to get a list of great emotional freedom techniques you can do while being guided.

#36 Be Your Own Guru

All too often we give up our personal power to others, and allow doctors; television programmes; magazine articles and many others to tell us what is good for us. This can quite easily lead to emotional overwhelm. In fact, you are the best person in your life to actually dictate what is best for you. If you learn to listen to your body's own signals you will be able to build a healthy lifestyle to support you body, mind and spirit. This is a fabulous little video on YouTube called "Be Your Own Guru" by Jonathan Fields. In it, he outlines just why this little tip is so important.

#37 What Advice Would You Give To A Friend?

This is emotional prosperity at its simplest. So many of us spend such a lot of time giving great advice to others, yet we seem to never take the same advice in our own lives! When we have something go wrong, or we feel blue try to remember that you are a fount of brilliant advice. Just flip the situation so it is happening to someone else. What would you suggest they try? Now – do that, your advice will be brilliant!

#38 Get A Pet!

Studies have shown that pet owners show considerably lower levels of stress and anxiety, feel less lonely and disconnected; and that just being around animals can have a soothing and calming effect.

#39 Take Action!

The key to move past emotional overwhelm is to take action. Even if the action you take is something as simple as calling a friend to get support, it has been shown that not dwelling on our concerns and doing something about them can turn our mood in a moment. This tip always reminds me of the serenity prayer, which I find a huge comfort to me, my favourite YouTube clip of this is "The Serenity Prayer Song" by The Serenity Prayer Project.

#40 This Too Shall Pass

One of the simplest ways to help you to control your emotions in the moment is to just simply intone this simple affirmation a few times. Every moment passes, and so will this one. You will get through it, and you will be stronger for doing so.

Chapter 4: Making Changes That Will Last A Lifetime

Making changes can be difficult. You have been doing things this way for most of your life, and probably feel that you are muddling along relatively well. The reason to get aware, to take control and to make changes is to stop coasting. I am presuming you picked up this book because you have had enough of just surviving and are in the mood to make changes that will have you thriving, but just reading is not enough. As we said in an earlier tip – you have to take the actions and put these things into practice. My best advice is to choose just one or two things to try at a time. Do them daily, and make sure that they are as habitual as cleaning your teeth for you before you add anything new in (presuming cleaning your teeth is a regular habit for you of course!).

#41 Get Decisive!

One of the things I have noticed over the years is that people who are emotionally stable are really good at making decisions, they do so calmly and once they have taken a decision they get busy taking action on it. They are pragmatic, and realize that even though they have taken a decision this doesn't mean that they can't change their mind if things do not work out the way that they hoped.

However people who struggle to maintain a balanced emotional existence often struggle to make decisions. They often find themselves going back and forth between options, looking endlessly at the pros and cons, until they are literally paralyzed by too much information.

Of course we need information to make decisions, but do not let your information gathering become the only part of the process you ever undertake. Our gut instincts are often the most accurate decision we can make for us, so try not to let yourself move too far away from this initial reaction.

#42 Say Yes To The Right Things!

This is such a simple tip! What are the things you currently say 'Yes!' to all the time? What do you currently say 'No!' to?

More often than not, if you are having issues with your emotional prosperity, the balance of these will be incorrect. You will probably notice that your answers to the first question are the things that cause you stress, tiredness, and anxiety – whereas the things you currently say no to are probably those which bring you happiness and pleasure.

Try saying 'Yes' to a few more things that will improve your mood on a daily basis and watch it transform your life and how you feel about it.

#43 Smile And Laugh Daily

Have you ever noticed how often children smile and laugh in a day? The experts seem to disagree on actual statistics, but they seem to be consistent when it comes to the belief that it is a vastly different amount to the average adult. Laughter can be an emotional and physical release, and can even have the effect of a full cardio-vascular workout. Add to that its ability to assist us to sleep better, feel more relaxed and just enjoy life more implementing laughter as a tool to improve your emotional wellbeing is probably a very good idea.

#44 Get Sociable!

People who interact with others regularly not only tend to feel less lonely and isolated, but also suffer less anxiety; less periods of low mood; and show healthier physical tendencies.

The best way to get sociable is to do it in person, spend time with family and friends; but you can write letters or emails; telephone or text; use social media; join clubs or a church. Just get out and about and get in touch with others whenever you can!

#45 Volunteering

This is such a wonderful way to improve your emotional wellbeing. Not only do you get a feel good factor from assisting a cause that matters a lot to you; but you get to become a part of something bigger than yourself; be around other like-minded people; and possibly learn new skills and information. Volunteering really is a great thing to do – even if you only have a few hours a month to devote you will get so much out of that time that it makes it absolutely worth your while to do so.

#46 Join a Club!

Being around like-minded people is one of life's absolute pleasures. Why not join a club; a book group; a dinner group; a church; or even attend a class locally on a subject you love. You don't have to be good at the skill to start with, nobody will expect you to be an expert. Just take along your passion and you will be welcomed with open arms.

#47 Stimulate Your Senses!

One of the things that really helps us, as humans, to feel connected to the world we live in, and therefore in balance with our environment and our own lives, is to get our senses involved in the way we live. Evidence shows that taking up sensory based hobbies can really improve our mood and help us to maintain emotional balance.

Why not try pottery, or give gardening a go? How about cooking, or trying new foods? Go for an aromatherapy massage or make perfume? Why not get out in nature and hug a tree, listen or play music, or even learn to knit or crochet?

Pick something that uses as many senses as you can – your sight; taste; touch; smell; and what you hear – involving your entire brain will help it to be healthier.

#48 Read A Good Book!

The ability to sit down, relax and lose yourself in a fantasy world is actually proven to be really good for us. Don't keep your reading for around the pool when you are on holiday – make it a part of your everyday life.

#49 Listen To, Or Play Music

Music can be highly uplifting, can help us to work out our angst and can even make us cry. No matter what emotion you need to feel and process there will be a piece of music that will help you to do so.

Why not build an emotions playlist? If you need to feel more relaxed choose some fantastically soothing tunes; if you want to release anger get some great angry ones; if you need to cry choose the saddest songs you know; and if you want to feel happy and on top of the world pick some incredible anthems that just make you smile!

#50 Get Playful!

As we move into adulthood, we often forget to schedule time into our day to enjoy play. But just because we are no longer children it shouldn't mean that we have to be grown up twenty four hours a day. As primates we learn from play, and this ability to spot patterns and put things together from doing so is one of the most incredible things about us as a genus. Rather than all your learning coming from sterile classrooms, why not have some fun?

Enjoy looking for ways to try and make what you do more fun, and your emotional prosperity will soar because you will get so much from every activity - if you are actually enjoying and learning from it.

#51 Take Baby Steps

When we begin to make changes in our lives it can be all too easy to take on too much all at once. This can mean that we find ouselves overwhelmed, and it is very common that good intentions to slip by the wayside. Try keeping it simple. Only tackle one change at a time, keep at it until it is a habit - and only add something new once it is!

#52 Build up an Image Store

If you are a regular on social media you will already be aware of the mood improving powers of a particular YouTube clip, or a well taken picture. We all have our favourites; mine are penguins, baby polar bears and hippos doing crazy things!

I can feel my mood lift dramatically just looking for a few moments at a picture or video that makes me smile. These are free and quick. Start to build your library of go-to images as quickly as you can!

#53 Affirmations

Affirmations are positive statements that you can repeat to yourself frequently, in order to replace and over-ride past, less supportive, thoughts and beliefs. Though I said earlier that these can be quite a long winded way to make changes, this doesn't mean that they aren't useful when used properly.

When done with passion, and especially if you include mirror work, they can be a beneficial part of your emotional prosperity workout. This YouTube clip "Improve Your Self-Esteem With Mirror Work and Positive Affirmations" by LifeWorksForYou will show you how to use affirmations effectively.

#54 Subliminal Messaging

This can be a really useful technique, and there are software programmes you can get so you can imbed phrases into your screensaver on your computer (Such as Subliminal Blaster), or record and mix them into your favourite music tracks (something simple to use like Audacity is useful).

These can blast affirmations and positive thoughts directly into the subconscious brain, so can really speed up any work you are doing using these.

#55 Visualisation

Visualisation is a really useful tool that you can indulge in whenever you need to. The basic premise is that you vividly imagine the outcome you wish to have occur. By doing so it is possible to 'trick' the brain that this is already a reality, so it sets up the pathways in the brain required to make sure it actually happens.

The brain finds it a little tricky to tell the difference between reality and a vividly imagined fantasy. This is in some ways a little worrying, but it is also one of those cracking shortcuts to making our brain work for us better. Make your daydreams vivid and full of sensory input, repeat them on permanent loop as often as you can. And your teachers said that daydreaming in class would get you nowhere!

#56 Deflect Hurtful Words

I love this technique and I use it all the time. When somebody says something offensive or hurtful, simply imagine the words/emotions/situation as a red ball coming your way. Then as it hits you, imagine it bouncing off you in a completely different direction and watch as it goes far away, or bounces off you with sufficient force to shatter it into tiny pieces!

#57 Meditation

There is little that meditation can't help with, and managing your emotions is just one of them. It is a truly great tool. This YouTube clip "How to Meditate ~Learn to Meditate in 5 Easy Steps" by Audio Entrainment Meditation Music and Binaural Beats is a great resource to help you to get started on this.

#58 Forgiveness

Most people when I mention this are a little confused. They often feel that the fact that they forgive everybody is possibly part of the problem. However, if they are forgetting to forgive themselves as well, then forgiveness is only half complete! You have to genuinely mean it too – and not just say you forgive someone when you don't really. When we don't genuinely forgive, we cannot let the situation causing us pain go, and therefore we will continue to relive it.

#59 Anchoring

Anchoring is an NLP tool and can be really useful to help us to change our emotions in a moment so that we can continue to cope, until we can safely process the emotions.

Simply think of a time when you have felt the feeling that you wish to be able to summon up on command. For example feeling happy; confident; successful; loving etc.

Take a few moments to really wallow in this memory, or a number of memories as you squeeze your thumb and a finger together (do not confuse your happy finger with your confident one – make sure they are different!). Feel the emotion in all its intensity. See what you saw, feel what you felt, smell what you smelt, hear what you heard.

Now, let your finger and thumb release and think about something completely different for a while.

Then squeeze the finger and thumb together again. You should get the happy feeling without having to go through the situation you once felt happy in. If, however your feeling of happiness or success is a little weedy, try doing it again, and really ramp up the intensity of the emotions as if you were turning up the volume knob on a stereo.

#60 Enjoy Visits To Your Own Cinema

Just take a moment to reflect on what is making you feel so low. I want you to imagine that you are watching it on the screen of a cinema. Pay attention to where in the cinema you are sitting, are you right up close to the screen (is the action right in your face) or do you feel so distant from it that it seems like it is happening to someone else?

Now, try moving where you are sitting in the cinema – move closer, or further away from the screen until you find a position where the situation no longer makes you feel bad.

#61 The Power Of Silly Voices

If you have been hurt or upset by a particular person then this little tip is really useful. Close your eyes for a moment and imagine that they are saying those hurtful things to you. Like in your cinema, note where they are – chances are they are right up close and in your face. If this is the case, then imagine them shrinking and getting further and further away from you; and enjoy laughing at them as they get smaller and smaller, and their voices get higher and more like a cartoon character.

#62 Swapsies

We have to get a little OCD about this one, but in a good way! You will need to pay close attention to as many of your thoughts as you can. You will be looking for all those negative little thoughts that just sneak in. If the statement is something you say regularly create a reframe – for example "I am so tired" could be reframed to "I have enough energy to do everything I need to". The statement does need to still be true, so your brain can believe it – but it should be a positive, glass half full approach!

#63 Use Your Brains!

Many of us have jobs, or hobbies that use only a few areas of our brains. We tend to focus on the types of skills that come naturally to us. By undertaking brain training options, so that we work out the whole of our brain, we can improve our emotional health and wellbeing. Apps are available, such as Peak (www.peak.net) that mean you can do just a few minutes a day. You will be delighted to see how much your brain improves in its agility – especially in areas that you previously thought weren't your area of expertise!

#64 Undertake Tasks With The Wrong Hand

Research has shown that just simply doing some easy tasks - such as writing; eating a meal etc. – with your non-dominant hand you can improve your mental agility as you will need to use different areas in your brain. The more areas you use of your brain, the healthier it is, the stronger the connections between the neurons, and so the more capable of withstanding stress your brain will be.

#65 Get Out Into Nature

There is a naturally calming effect that happens when we get out and spend time in the great outdoors. Whether you simply plant up a window box, or are lucky enough to have great scenery to take long walks on your doorstep it is a really good idea to take part in nature. Grow things, walk barefoot – but most importantly make sure you spend at least 15 to 20 minutes a day outside so your body can synthesize sufficient Vitamin D to keep your brain healthy!

Chapter 5: Keep On Moving So Your Success Continues

So far we have included lots of techniques that you can use as one offs, or build together into a regular practice. If you really want to improve your emotional prosperity, then it is really important to build a practice that works for you, that is easy enough to fit around your daily life so that you will stick to it. This means making sure you do enough to have an impact, but keep it manageable enough that you can continue to it, even on those days when you just cannot be bothered. Hopefully the techniques in this chapter will help you to make this a regular habit that you will love and enjoy.

#66 Build A Morning Routine

Experts all seem to agree that if you want to build a new habit into your life, the best time to do the activity required is first thing in the morning. This basically helps because it stops the anxiety of trying to find time in a busy day to fit it in, or the possibility of skipping your practice because you are tired or can't be bothered at the end of your day.

Maybe choose a combination of 5 minutes of meditation; reframing a situation that has been worrying you; and spending five minutes thinking about things that you are grateful for. This simple routine would take no more than fifteen minutes, but could drastically improve how well your day goes.

#67 Create An Evening Routine

As you have started your day so positively, why not end it that way too. By creating a regular evening practice you not only end your day reflecting on something positive, but it can help you to improve your sleep too.

Maybe try 5 minutes of deep breathing; a guided meditation; and a few minutes visualising how you want your tomorrow to work out!

#68 Get A Mentor

A mentor can really help you to stay on track. You can learn from their experiences, and pick up new techniques and skills – as well as having a friendly and supportive ear to help you out when you need it.

#69 Be Empathetic

It can be very important to remember that the reason someone else may be reacting to us in a negative way may have nothing whatsoever to do with us and our behaviour towards them. By being more aware that other people have issues that they are dealing with too, we can often diffuse the way in which we react to many situations.

I taught a client this simple tip and, within ten minutes of leaving me, she went to the supermarket where a women slammed a trolley into her, and then proceeded to get grumpy that my client didn't apologise to her (for being in her way presumably!) My client remembered what we had been talking about, and rather than letting the incident play on her mind for hours, and assuming that she had in fact been in the wrong - as she would have done in the past - she simply assumed that the other woman had been having a tough day, sent her forgiveness in her mind and found that she was able to move on and do her shopping with a happy heart.

#70 Let It Go!

This is the simplest of advice, but often the hardest to master. The way to ensure that we can do this is to remember that we live in the moment. What has already happened, or what may happen later today, really doesn't have any relevance to us right now. If we can find a way to accept that the past is gone, if we can learn the lesson that the events were there to teach us, then letting go of it is easier.

For example, how easily do you let happy memories drift away? They usually take just a little bit longer for most people to search out in the memory. Yet, those negative ones, the ones where we got hurt, or someone did something terrible to us – they come back so easily. This is because we do let go of positive things, they haven't harmed us and so it is easy to do so. But if you can establish a purpose for the pain or feelings of inadequacy etc. then letting go of them is so much easier to do because they will have a valuable purpose that you can take forward to help you in your life.

#71 Dealing With Critics

It is difficult to deal with critics in the moment, but once we are away from them we can quickly ask a few simple questions to establish if what they are saying has any real power over you. None of us want hurtful words or actions playing through our heads all day, so use these to help you.

What exactly was said? Is it true? Who said it? How much does their good opinion really matter to you? Would anybody who genuinely knows and loves you say the same thing?

It is really important that we don't give our personal power to others – especially if they are people whose good opinion really isn't important in our life!

#72 There Is No Such Thing As Failure

As long as you learn from something a Fail is simply your First Attempt In Learning.

Edison took thousands of attempts to create the electric light bulb and not once did he consider that he had failed. He knew that he had simply found another thing that didn't create it so knew he needed to try something new.

#73 Until You Die, It Is Not The End

As the wonderful hotel owner in The Best Marigold Hotel tells us so wisely, 'everything will be alright out in the end, and if everything is not alright, then it cannot be the end'. Try to remember that Effort Never Dies and the 'end' will lose its sting.

#74 No Does Not Mean This is The End!

No is not necessarily a denial. To the most successful in our society no simply means it is time to move on to our Next Opportunity!

Don't let a no hold you down and make you think you can't do it, or you aren't good enough. It simply means that one person could not see your potential – there will be somebody else out there who will.

#75 Learn To Be Patient

This links in with developing empathy for other people's situations. When we appreciate that others have problems too, it is much easier to be patient with them.

Also, when we are prepared to accept that just because we don't get our wants and needs immediately, that it doesn't automatically mean that we never will, we can enjoy the journey much more.

#76 10 Years From Now…

We often joke that in a few years that we may look back and laugh about difficult situations, and this is often true – however it is probably even more useful to take a few moments and imagine exactly how important this moment may be to you in ten years time.

When I do this with clients, I often get them to imagine what happens in ten years if they do nothing about how they feel. Then I get them to imagine it again, but this time to focus on how it may be if they just make a few changes, and then again if they make a lot of changes.

Often, the difference between these two possible futures can be enough to help you to at least commit to making a few minor changes – even if trying to do everything in this book feels overwhelming!

#77 Be Yourself – You Are Enough, Just The Way You Are

Hopefully this is pretty self explanatory – but just in case! Okay, so you aren't perfect, and you do make mistakes. But you now know that as long as you learn from them, and keep on trying that things will improve for you.

You do not have to impress anybody else on the planet – in fact you are loved and appreciated by many people already just the way you are. Try and look at yourself through the eyes of your best friend. He or she would not have chosen you to fulfil that role if you weren't worthy of it.

Trust the opinions of those who love you – not those who barely know you, even if you are your greatest naysayer. Ignore that little voice in your head that says you aren't okay as you are – it lies!

#78 Expand Your Comfort Zone

Most of us live within a very tight little space, we give ourselves no room to breathe even it can be so restrictive. Now, it is important to have a space where you feel safe, but you shouldn't remain in it at all times.

Start small: for example if you currently rarely leave the house, why not try just walking to the end of your drive for a few days; then push that boundary and try going to a local store and so on. Build up gradually, and get comfortable with each step as you take it.

If you are an adrenaline junky, constantly pushing the boundaries – parachuting from planes or bungeeing off cliffs, you can skip this tip!

#79 If You Set Goals, Do So Wisely

Goal setting is a very useful thing to do – but only if it doesn't become yet another thing you use to beat yourself up with. When you set goals, make sure that you pick a wide range of short, medium and long term goals; set realistic time scales in which to achieve them; and most importantly make sure some goals are really easy, some are a little tough, and some will stretch you outside your comfort zone! One of my favourite programs for doing my own personal goal setting is Goals on Track.

#80 Make Sure Your Goals Are What You Want!

I once undertook a goal setting exercise, and I wrote down a huge range of lifestyle, material object, physical and financial goals. What I forgot to do was to ensure that they were actually things I truly wanted! When you set a goal, you should be excited about the idea of achieving it; you should be happy to make the time that you will need to do so; and you should find taking the steps to do so a pleasure. If any of these are missing, you are probably just chasing this goal because you think you should.

Don't beat yourself up about time wasted, just stop – and move onwards to something that does get your passion up!

#81 Monitor Your Self Talk

When I first started my self help journey, I was absolutely my worst critic and the biggest bully in the playground! I have learnt that it is really important to be encouraging and supportive of myself as I try and make changes in my life – shaming and guilt will never help you. You are a great person, so start being a little kinder – especially when you are just talking to yourself.

#82 Build A Spiritual Basis For Your Life

Now, I am not automatically talking about getting religion here. Spirituality is a very personal thing that is essentially all about forging a connection with the world around us. When we do so we find ourselves much more content, our emotions are more balanced and our physical health even improves. Explore the many and varied options – or even just get out into nature to appreciate the beauty and magnificence all around you.

#83 The Power Of Your Thoughts!

A really interesting study, that is detailed in this article "Marriage Math" by Hara Estroff Marrano, showed that there is a definite ratio between the number of positive statements, versus the number of negative ones made between married couples that can actually predict the probability of that relationship succeeding. This proves that feeling valued and appreciated is key to ensuring longevity in a relationship.

You are in a relationship with yourself and you need to be just as careful about your positive to negative ratio as you would be when nurturing a relationship with someone else - if you want your body and mind to continue to deliver the results that you desire.

#84 Tackle Your Phobias And Fears

Any anxiety is dangerous to the balance of chemicals in our brains, and the rest of our bodies. When we actually stand up to our fears and take action, we can move past them. If doing so alone seems too daunting, then you can try various different therapies: EFT; Hypnotherapy; CBT; and NLP all have some great results when tackling fear and phobias so you can move forward in your life without them.

Chapter 6: How To Ensure Your Physical Health Impacts Your Emotional Health The Right Way!

I have talked a lot throughout this book about the importance that our mental health and wellbeing has on our physical health, and vice versa. We are complex beings – made up of a number of elements – and it is vital that we pay close attention to maintaining homeostasis for all of these – physically, mentally, and spiritually. I have a number of clients who notice a massive difference to how good they feel when their hydration or nutrition is below their personal, optimal levels. I personally find that I can notice a drop in positivity when I miss my daily walk. So here are my favorite tips on how to make sure you look after your physical health, to have the most impact on your emotional wellbeing.

#85 See A Therapist

This may seem like it is all about your mental and emotional health, but seeing a therapist – be that a psychotherapist; a massage therapist; a reflexologist or whatever your choice of holistic treatment may be – will assist you in your journey towards holistic wellbeing.

A therapist can act as a mentor, as a place to unburden our worries, and someone who can deliver a treatment that helps us to relax, and rejuvenate.

#86 Relax!

Our way of life seems to be a permanent competition of who can do more, be more and have more. We rush around constantly; and forget to give our body the time it needs to heal and repair, and our brains the time they need to process all the experiences we are having. We need this time, to unwind and be comfortable in our own skins in order to maintain the homeostasis that we require to stay healthy – so take time to chill out!

#87 Physical Changes Come First

More often than not we will notice the physical changes in our bodies, before we are aware of the impact our actions may be having on our mind and emotions. Often when we are experiencing the beginnings of changes to our emotional wellbeing we might be more prone to colds and infections; when we are anxious we may display muscle tension; headaches; digestive issues; rapid breathing; and increased blood pressure.

If in doubt as to the cause of your physical symptoms, just try slowing down a little, breathing deeply and making sure you have whatever you need to ensure that you can care for your physical symptoms as naturally as you can. Once you feel a little brighter, then it is the time to look at what was happening in your life before you felt pain or fell ill. Use some of the tips in this book to help you to create a more balanced way of looking at it, and work out what you can learn from it all.

#88 Take A Break!

We are all busy, we all have lots of things to get done – and that means many of us believe that we don't have any time to stop and take a break!

We are a little bit short term when it comes to the ability to focus on a single task (about 45 minutes); after this time, even if you are working ridiculously hard you may not be getting as much from that work as you were in that initial 45 minutes. When you schedule a 5 to 15 minute break every 45 minutes you will find that you will get more done; will understand more; and therefore you will be more productive!

#89 Get Active!

The best thing to do, in that little break that you take every 45 minutes, is to get active. Activity improves blood flow; helps to promote the production of the chemicals that reduce stress and anxiety within our bodies; and keeps our muscles supple and toned. Why not run up the stairs, do some yoga stretches, or even just walk outside for a few minutes?

#90 Get Hydrated!

Our brains are approximately 80-85% water and our body is around 70-75%. If either has insufficient hydration to undertake its necessary functions, you will experience low mood, sluggishness and even a reduced immune system and impaired digestion. If you wait until you are thirsty, you are already dehydrated, so sip at some fresh water throughout the day to improve your energy and mental clarity.

#91 Nutrition For Mood

Like everything else in our body, our brain needs specific nutrition in order for it to work well. If our body is flooded with adrenaline and the other 'stimulating' hormones it can be difficult for our body to produce sufficient 'calming' ones for us to feel content. We don't run away from our stressors these days, so we need to make sure that we do not overload our systems with extra stimulants and anti-nutrients. To ensure you have good brain health you need to follow exactly the same guidelines that would produce a healthy body.

It is good to limit or avoid: sugar; saturated fats and too many processed foods.

It is good to include lots of green leafy vegetables; oily fish; salads and other water rich fruits and vegetables. Try and choose organic if you can, but choose the best quality food that you can afford.

Patrick Holford submitted a great article about the benefits of nutrition on mental wellbeing that was published here, on the <u>Institute of Optimum Nutrition</u> website.

#92 Supplements For The Brain

Vitamin C; B Vitamins – especially B6; Magnesium and Chromium can often be taken as supplements to improve mental and emotional health. There are other options, such as 5-HTP; Gingko Biloba; Green Tea; Guarana; and many others which may help, but it is always best to consult a qualified nutritionist and/or herbalist to establish your personal requirements. Choose someone who can test properly for deficiencies and understands your symptom picture well.

#93 Regular Exercise

Exercise makes you feel great! It helps us to regulate the stimulating hormones (adrenaline, noradrenaline and cortisone) and stimulate the production of those that we require to kill pain; regulate appetite; and improve the way we feel. It helps every system of the body to function more effectively and boosts confidence. Research has even shown that a simple, daily walk can be more effective than medication to reduce the symptoms of mild to moderate depression and other mood disorders.

Choose an activity you love and you will never struggle to make a date, two to three times a week, to get a bit hot and sweaty and have some fun!

#94 Get Good Sleep

Many people struggle to sleep well. Often uncomfortable beds and too much stress can make it very difficult to drop off. But sleep is vital so that our brain can process all the experiences of the day, and to undertake the necessary repairs to our cells that it cannot do when energy is required by our brains and digestive systems.

Good Sleep Hygiene can make a real difference to how well you sleep – and that will make a difference to every aspect of your wellbeing.

1. Your bedroom is for one thing, sleep (okay, you can have sex in there too if you have a willing partner!) Get the TV, your mobile phone; the laptop or tablet and any other electrical appliances out of it.

2. Go to bed when you are genuinely tired.

3. Get up at exactly the same time every day.

4. Ensure that the room is dark and that it is at a comfortable temperature – being too hot or too cold will affect how well you sleep.

If you still struggle to drop off, try to avoid sleeping pills. Consult a qualified naturopath for herbal remedies or homeopathic options that may help. Sleeping tablets can seem a good idea, but they can be addictive, and studies are showing that the sleep which they provide isn't conducive to creating the healing environment within your body that regular sleep does.

#95 Plan Your Day

Many of us have a to-do list, but few of us actually work out how much time we think each item might take - and whether it is realistic that we will be able to fit everything we have put on it, into the time we have available. Making a realistic plan can really help to prevent overwhelm; give structure to your day; and help you to realize which items are genuinely important.

I have items that have been at the bottom of my to-do list for over ten years. They aren't important to my day to day life, and so until they become so that is exactly where they will stay!

#96 Prioritize Healthy Activities

If you are anything like I once was - and most of my clients over the years have been - you probably fit in your healthy activities around everything else in your life. Your trip to the gym may happen if you can fit it in between dropping your son at badminton and picking your daughter up from Girl Scouts; going to the health food store to get supplements will happen if you have time in your lunch break; making a home cooked meal will happen if you get in from work on time and so on.

One of my clients used just these excuses for why she couldn't come to see me; go to yoga; or eat anything that wasn't processed or from a fast food restaurant. She recently began to plan her week around her pilates and yoga classes, and has been amazed at how much more energy and time she seems to have – even though she is now actually doing more things.

Get the things that keep you healthy at the top of your list, and you will feel better, be more prosperous, and more productive.

#97 Dance When You Do The Housework!

When we try to find the fun in chores and activities we dislike, if we can find a way to have those boring aspects of our life have more meaning; and bring us more connection to our loved ones, we will be much more likely to do them.

I am like most people, I dislike doing my household chores. Like me, I am sure that you know someone else who adores doing them. I once asked my friend why, and she told me it was because she feels close to her family when she does these things for them. She gets a real buzz out of creating a healthy and happy environment for her family to live in. I realized that I needed to either employ her to clean my home, or find a way to get some of that fabulous connection. I found that dancing to songs, especially if they bring back great memories to my mind of times spent with family and friends, as I do my chores makes it a much more enjoyable task. This makes it less overwhelming, I get less anxious when I think about doing it, and it is a great workout too!

There may be some things in your life that would be difficult to dance to – but try and find some way to make the boring 'should do' stuff a bit more fun, find a way for it to have more meaning and then it won't be so hard to knuckle down to it.

#98 Get A Dose Of Sunshine Every Day

Sunlight lifts our mood, even when the sun is behind clouds! There is a beautiful world outside your door, enjoy it while you can.

#99 Avoid Alcohol!

Alcohol is a confusing drug. When we first drink it, it can improve our mood – but it is in fact a depressant, and if you want to maintain emotional wellbeing it is best avoided. The impact of even one or two drinks can be enough to affect sleep and mood for up to a week after it has been consumed.

#100 Don't Smoke Or Drink Too Much Caffeine!

Nicotine and Caffeine are both very strong stimulants, and can affect our body chemistry drastically, making it difficult for us to relax and get sufficient deep sleep. Caffeine is also a diuretic, so can take vital hydration from our systems. For many people it is best to avoid it all together, but if you do want to include it, set yourself a cut off of midday – then switch to caffeine free drinks, ideally water to quench your thirst.

Cigarettes are damaging to every aspect of our health and wellbeing, and smoking is a known risk factor for stroke; heart disease; and cancers– if you can get some help to quit then do so. The impact on your wellbeing in the mid to long term will be well worth any discomfort you may go through in the short term.

Conclusion

Well, we have reached the end of this "Top 100", I hope that you have found some great tips, techniques and tools to help you to improve your emotional prosperity.

There are many more ways to help you to balance your emotions, to improve your physical and mental health, but this list will give you more than a great start. Try and enjoy building a morning and evening routine; and take time to build a life that helps you to feel great. Look after your nutrition, find a way of moving your body that you can enjoy and want to do regularly; and get aware of your triggers and your reactions – both physical and emotional – to things. The more awareness you have, the more likely you will be able to take preventative measures to ensure you maintain homeostasis of both your mental and physical health.

Remember that your emotions are not good or bad, they are just emotions, and they are there – just like a physical symptom – to let us know that there is something that we need to pay attention to. It is you who determines how you will react to your emotions and situations in life. Learn from your emotions, use them wisely and you will find your prosperity, contentment and joy.

I hope this book was able to help you to learn some really useful ways to improve your mood and manage your emotions

The next step is to take action, and choose your favorite three things from this book to start working on! Once these have been mastered, choose three more and continue your journey until you are truly the master of your emotions!

Finally, if you discovered at least one thing that has helped you or that you think would be beneficial to someone else, be sure to take a few seconds to easily post a quick positive review. As an author, your positive feedback is desperately needed. Your highly valuable five star reviews are like a river of golden joy flowing through a sunny forest of mighty trees and beautiful flowers! *To do your good deed in making the world a better place by helping others with your valuable insight, just leave a nice review.*

![Thanks and Best of Luck]

My Other Books and Audio Books
www.AcesEbooks.com

Peak Performance Books

SUCCESS
SUCCESS STRATEGIES
THE TOP 100 BEST WAYS TO BE SUCCESSFUL

Ace McCloud

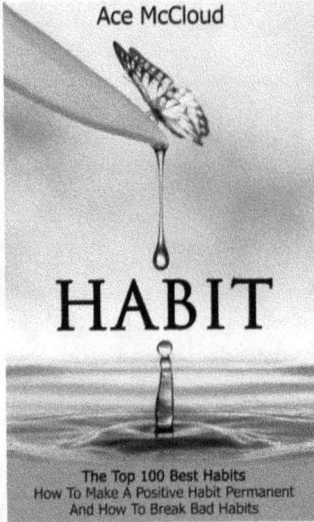

Ace McCloud

HABIT

The Top 100 Best Habits
How To Make A Positive Habit Permanent
And How To Break Bad Habits

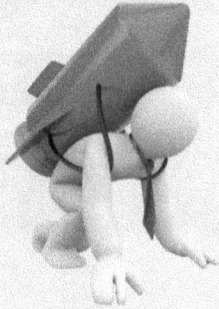

MOTIVATION
MASTER THE POWER OF MOTIVATION
TO PROPEL YOURSELF TO SUCCESS

Ace McCloud

ATTITUDE
Discover The True Power Of
A Positive Attitude

Ace McCloud

SELF DISCIPLINE
Unleash The Power Of Self Discipline,
Influence And Willpower In Your Life
To Achieve Anything

Ace McCloud

Competitive Strategies
WINNING STRATEGIES
The Top 100 Best Strategies
For Peak Performance During Competitions

Ace McCloud

Health Books

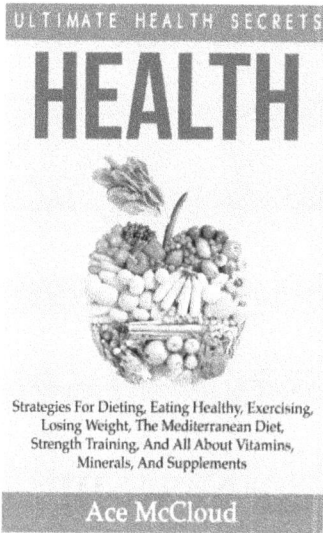

ULTIMATE HEALTH SECRETS

HEALTH

Strategies For Dieting, Eating Healthy, Exercising, Losing Weight, The Mediterranean Diet, Strength Training, And All About Vitamins, Minerals, And Supplements

Ace McCloud

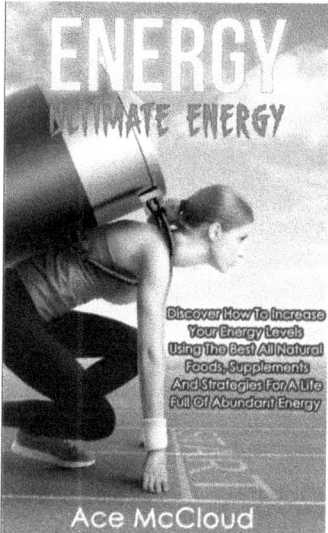

ENERGY
ULTIMATE ENERGY

Discover How To Increase Your Energy Levels Using The Best All Natural Foods, Supplements And Strategies For A Life Full Of Abundant Energy

Ace McCloud

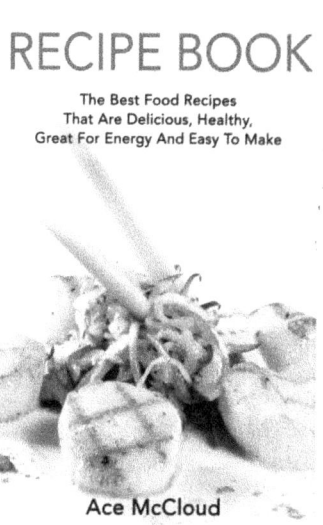

RECIPE BOOK

The Best Food Recipes That Are Delicious, Healthy, Great For Energy And Easy To Make

Ace McCloud

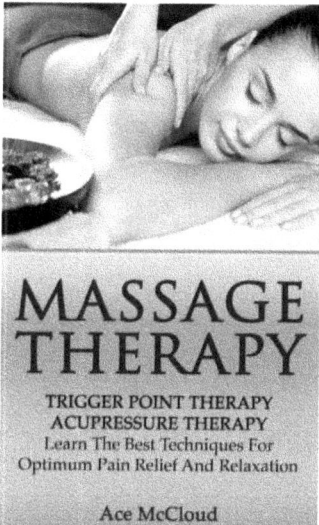

MASSAGE THERAPY

TRIGGER POINT THERAPY
ACUPRESSURE THERAPY
Learn The Best Techniques For
Optimum Pain Relief And Relaxation

Ace McCloud

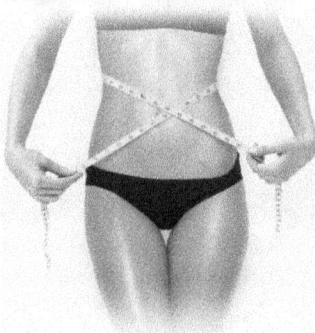

LOSE WEIGHT

THE TOP 100 BEST WAYS
TO LOSE WEIGHT QUICKLY AND HEALTHILY

Ace McCloud

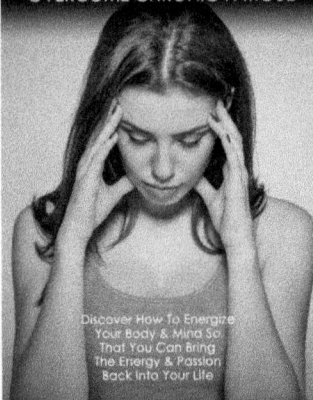

FATIGUE
OVERCOME CHRONIC FATIGUE

Discover How To Energize
Your Body & Mind So
That You Can Bring
The Energy & Passion
Back Into Your Life

Ace McCloud

Be sure to check out my audio books as well!

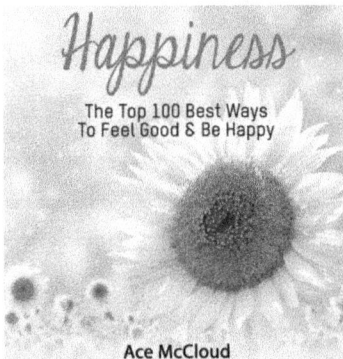

Happiness

The Top 100 Best Ways
To Feel Good & Be Happy

Ace McCloud

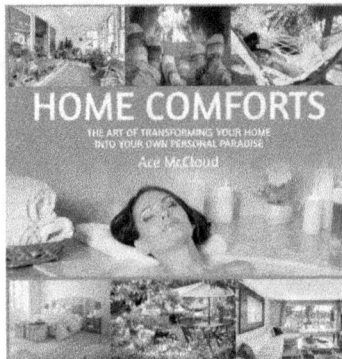

HOME COMFORTS
THE ART OF TRANSFORMING YOUR HOME
INTO YOUR OWN PERSONAL PARADISE

Ace McCloud

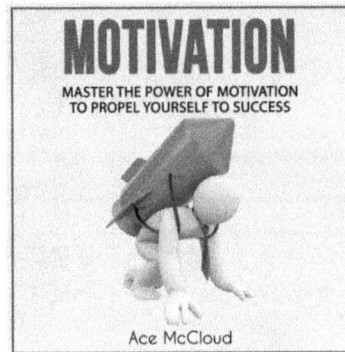

MOTIVATION
MASTER THE POWER OF MOTIVATION
TO PROPEL YOURSELF TO SUCCESS

Ace McCloud

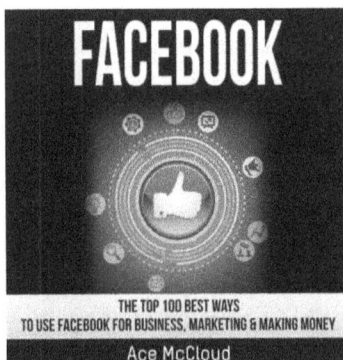

FACEBOOK

THE TOP 100 BEST WAYS
TO USE FACEBOOK FOR BUSINESS, MARKETING & MAKING MONEY

Ace McCloud

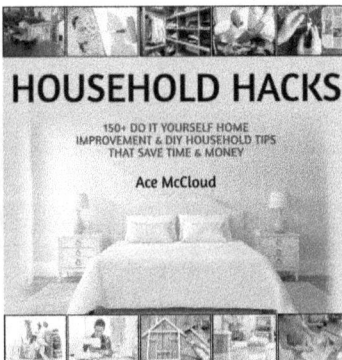

HOUSEHOLD HACKS

150+ DO IT YOURSELF HOME
IMPROVEMENT & DIY HOUSEHOLD TIPS
THAT SAVE TIME & MONEY

Ace McCloud

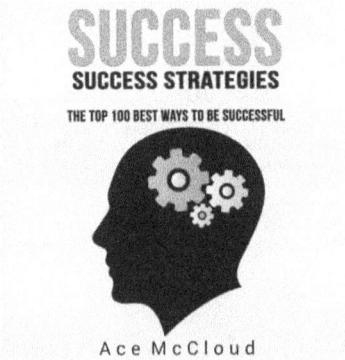

SUCCESS
SUCCESS STRATEGIES

THE TOP 100 BEST WAYS TO BE SUCCESSFUL

Ace McCloud

Check out my website at: **www.AcesEbooks.com** for a complete list of all of my books and high quality audio books. I enjoy bringing you the best knowledge in the world and wish you the best in using this information to make your journey through life better and more enjoyable! **Best of luck to you!**

www.ingramcontent.com/pod-product-compliance
Lightning Source LLC
Chambersburg PA
CBHW080631030426
42336CB00018B/3151